# Massachusetts Elder Crisis Law

## How You Can Help Your Parent or Loved One

Second Edition

By John T. Gosselin
Member, National Academy of Elder Law Attorneys

Copyright © 2018 Gosselin & Kyriakidis PC
All Rights Reserved

# Contents

INTRODUCTION ................................................................. 1

SECTION ONE: Crash Course in Massachusetts
    Elder Law .................................................. 7

SECTION TWO: Frequently Asked Questions About
    Elder Crisis Law ....................................... 25

SECTION THREE: The Adult Child's Survival Guide:
    How to Give Good Care and
    Live Your Life at the Same Time ........ 63

SECTION FOUR: Finding and Working With A
    Qualified Massachusetts Elder
    Care Law Firm ........................................ 77

CONCLUSION ................................................................. 87

DISCLAIMER .................................................................. 89

# Introduction

*Mountains cannot be surmounted except
by winding paths.
– Johann Wolfgang Von Goethe*

If you are an adult with parents experiencing an elder law crisis in Massachusetts, this guidebook of frequently asked questions will help you navigate the difficult decisions and uncertain path ahead.

For instance, perhaps your father fell and hurt himself while tinkering in the garage. As you talked with him further and discussed the incident with his primary care physician, you came to the alarming realization that he is in the early stages of dementia. The revelation touched off a complex suite of emotions, including anxiety about the diagnosis and confusion about how to handle things, logistically and financially. This reference book will give you resources to help your dad with tax matters and health decisions and help you get clearer about your own role in his care.

Alternatively, maybe you're a mother in your 40s who's caring for young children while also attending to your parents. Being part of the "Sandwich Generation" is never easy, even in the best of times. But perhaps you just discovered that your sick mom's finances and retirement plans are in complete disarray. Among other things, she needs to move assets to create an income stream through annuities that the state can't touch. You want to assist her *and* care for your own kids *and* (somehow) find time and space to meet your own needs. This book will give you tools and strategies along those lines.

Our legal team works with children of senior parents all the time to create sensitive, strategic solutions to elder crisis problems. We understand the roller coaster of emotions that you are likely experiencing as well as the urgency with which you must act. Below, we'll explain the mission of this book and summarize what's to come - all in the service of helping you enjoy more clarity and peace of mind.

## Section One: A Crash Course on Massachusetts Elder Crisis Law

This "101" course will introduce important terminology and ideas, laying out definitions in an easy-to-understand format. For instance, we'll discuss MassHealth: what it is, why it exists, what it covers, etc. We'll review the five-year lookback period in detail and provide links to outside resources that you can access for more information. We'll provide a simple overview of trusts and annuities and how they should operate as well as capital gains taxes, gift taxes, estate taxes, powers of attorney, health care proxies and many more critical ideas, so you have the vocabulary you need to understand your role in the process.

## Section Two: Frequently Asked Questions About Elder Crisis Law

We'll unpack common questions that adult children have about the process. For instance: Why is it important to have a power of attorney signed before a senior is incompetent? What are Massachusetts Health Qualifying annuities, and why are they important? What's the difference between for profit and non-profit nursing homes, and what do I need to know about nursing home care in general? What if I suspect senior abuse or neglect? How do you qualify for state coverage?

## Section Three: The Adult Child's Survival Guide: How to Give Good Care and Live Your Life at the Same Time

Many adult children (typically between 40 and 65) face a bundle of conflicts when caring for their elderly parents and getting the family through crisis. We will identify and address the most common and vexing of these issues. For instance, how should you take care of your children when you're busy putting out fires related to your parents? What if you live hundreds of miles from Massachusetts? What if your job doesn't offer much flexibility? How should you deal with depression, anxiety and other emotions triggered by your parent's crisis? What should YOU change about your approach to financial and medical planning, based on what's happening with your folks?

## Section Four: Finding and Working with a Qualified Massachusetts Elder Crisis Law Firm

We'll go over how to recruit an attorney, how to find a firm whose values resonate with your own, what questions to ask during your consultation and how to make a smart decision when it comes to retaining a firm. We'll also talk about what to do and what not to do to make the relationship effective, especially when it comes to communicating with your attorney and team.

We hope this guidebook eases your stress and gives you new insight into the challenges and opportunities that await you. For immediate help dealing with your elder law crisis, please call the team at Gosselin & Kyriakidis, P.C for a confidential and free consultation at (781) 782-6000 or explore www.gosselinlaw.com to learn more about us, how we help Massachusetts families and why we do what we do.

SECTION ONE

# Crash Course in Massachusetts Elder Law

*The longer I live, the more beautiful life becomes.*
*— Frank Lloyd Wright*

**1. What is MassHealth?** The federal Medicare program provides elders with financial assistance to subsidize the costs of medical bills and prescription drugs. However, Medicare does not cover placement in a nursing home. On the other hand, Medicaid, called MassHealth in the Commonwealth is a joint program with the federal government that pays for nursing home placement for qualifying individuals.

**2. Why does it exist?** MassHealth gives health care coverage to more than a million people in the commonwealth, including seniors. The plan subsidizes all or part of health care premiums and pays for benefits, such as doctor visits, therapy, hospital stays, rehabilitation, and substance abuse and behavioral health services.

**3. Who qualifies?** MassHealth considers income and assets when determining whether a person is eligible for coverage.

**4. What is the five-year lookback period?** The five-year lookback period reviews a MassHealth applicant's finances. Federal laws changed in 2005, so that certain applicants can be disqualified in some cases. Previously, the applicant had to disclose transfers of real estate or assets within the previous 60 months to an irrevocable trust or within 36 months to a person.

Under the new federal law, the Deficit Reduction Act (DRA), the lookback period for personal asset transfers increased to 60 months, while the lookback period to an irrevocable trust remained unchanged. In addition, the applicant cannot give away assets for less than their fair market value during this time without incurring a penalty that includes ineligibility in MassHealth, based on the monthly cost of the nursing home.

Previously, the disqualification period started the same day that the person transferred the funds. So if your father transferred $50,000 each to you and your brother, the lookback period would total 10 months, if the nursing home cost $10,000 monthly. After that time, your father would be approved for MassHealth as long as he met the other criteria.

However, the DRA now changes the start date for the penalty period until the date that the nursing home resident has exhausted other resources and has applied for MassHealth. This means that, right when the elderly person most needs the benefits, he or she must wait out the penalty period.

In the past, your father would have been eligible by Nov. 1, 2016, if he gave you both the money on Jan. 1, 2016. But under the new rules, if your dad is healthy, that 10-month waiting period remains in limbo until he needs to use the benefit. If he suffers a head injury on Jan. 1, 2017, and he is admitted to a nursing home on Feb. 1, 2017, he will not qualify until Dec. 1, 2017.

To prevent disqualification, seniors must carefully consider how they will structure their finances and allow enough time to lapse if they plan to give money to family members, so that they do not risk losing coverage when benefits are needed most.

**5. What other resources can you suggest?** For additional information, check out the following resources.

  A. The 2015 Elder Education Program from the Massachusetts Bar Association is a handy resource with additional information on elder law.

    B. The MassHealth website.
    C. The Massachusetts Senior Care Association.
    D. The Executive Office on Elder Affairs.

### 6. What is a trust?

A trust is a fiduciary document that allows a person or organization, known as the *trustee*, to hold and manage assets on behalf of *beneficiaries*. (The trustee can also be the person creating the trust.)

Trusts offer diverse benefits. For instance, a trust can protect assets from so-called "creditors and predators" and reduce taxes on an estate, since the trust does not need to go through probate. Financial matters related to the estate also can remain private; by contrast, when you use a will, the process becomes a matter of public record. Trusts help clients with tax planning, transferring wealth to designated recipients and charities.

### 7. What are some examples of trusts that can be established?

**Irrevocable life insurance trust** (ILIT). The ILIT often is exempt from estate taxes for the beneficiary. In addition, creditors cannot place claims on these funds, and at least some — if not all — of the premiums can be paid by the trust, allowing you to decrease the taxable portion of the estate.

**Revocable living trust**. A revocable living trust protects assets in an account in the event that the account holder can no longer make financial decisions. This trust specifies terms for how beneficiaries can spend the money. Since the trust is revocable, you can change its terms relatively easily. The trust maker (e.g. your parent) thus enjoys a great deal of flexibility. Upon your parent's death, a trustee will then manage the account, and the funds will not have to go through the probate process.

**Charitable remainder trust**. A charitable trust allows your parent to donate to his or her favorite charity or cause upon death. A Charitable Remainder Unitrust pays a specific percentage to the recipient each year as income. A Charitable Remainder Annuity Trust specifies a dollar amount, paid to the recipient, which stays the same throughout the life of the trust. Creating these types of trusts can also lead to generous tax deductions.

**Supplemental needs trust (SNT)**. (We describe these trusts in greater detail in our answer to question 9.)

### 8. What are annuities?

An annuity is a type of insurance product that you purchase all at once (lump sum) or pay for over time. In return, you receive regular payouts (disbursements) according to a set schedule.

Annuities can shield your savings or create an income stream for you. Annuities allow you to plan for long-term care without risking funds, if you do not use the plan.

They can also be quite helpful when planning for Medicaid related challenges. For instance, let's say your parent needs help paying for a nursing home, but your parent's assets exceed the maximum allowable amount to qualify for government assistance, or he or she needs to enter a nursing home during Medicaid's five-year lookback period. Annuities could help. They could provide funds to pay for your parent's nursing home if he or she needs to wait out a penalty period.

An annuity can also reduce savings to the maximum allowable - about $120,000 for married couples - to allow one partner to qualify for Medicaid, so that he or she can be admitted to a nursing home. In this case, the healthy spouse receives an income stream but does not need to pay a penalty to transfer assets.

**Hybrid annuity policies** combine a long-term-care rider with an insurance policy. The IRS has passed laws allowing holders to use this money tax-free when paying for long-term care. Annuity income is not taxed, but if the holder cashes out the annuity, then the money is taxed. The purchaser puts money — at least $50,000 — into the annuity. The purchaser can also fund the annuity with a life insurance policy, and he or she can determine the amount and length of the coverage. He or she can also include or reject inflation coverage, which affects the plan's valuation.

Annuities generally increase in value at a compound interest rate and mature after a period of time (e.g. 20 years). The holder can use the annuity to pay for long-term care insurance. However, if your parent does not need to go to a nursing home, he or she can withdraw funds upon maturity or allow the annuity to continue to accrue interest as the policy remains in effect. Upon death, beneficiaries receive either the initial investment less monies paid toward long-term care or the value of the annuity, whichever is greater.

## 9. What is a Supplemental Needs Trust (SNT)?

Your parent might want to leave money to a disabled child or grandchild who cannot handle his or her own affairs. A supplemental needs trust, sometimes called a special needs trust, creates a process to transfer assets - such as an inheritance or proceeds from a personal injury lawsuit - in a way that does not disqualify the beneficiary from receiving public assistance benefits.

These trusts pay for expenses above and beyond daily bills, such as vacations, furniture, therapy and camp, and they provide the parent with peace of mind that the dependent's needs will be addressed.

**10. What are capital gains taxes?**
When you sell any type of property, such as a home, furniture or stocks, you will either sell it at a capital loss or a capital gain. The IRS categorizes capital gains into short-term (those held for less than a year) and long-term (those held for more than a year). The federal government generally taxes you at a maximum of 15 percent for most capital gains. You might not pay any capital gains tax if you are in a lower tax bracket. However, if you fall in the highest tax bracket, you could pay up to 20 percent in capital gains.

**11. What are gift taxes?**
Whenever you give someone a gift that exceeds the maximum allowable exclusion amount, set at $14,000 for individuals and $28,000 for couples annually in 2016, you need to pay a gift tax. There are a few general exceptions to this principle - for instance, if you give a gift to a spouse, pay college tuition for a grandchild, and or donate to a qualifying political or charitable organization. The IRS defines a "gift" as something of value given without the expectation of services or products provided in return. In most cases, the giver pays the gift tax.

If you lend your parent money, ask him or her to sign an actual loan agreement, preferably notarized, before you provide any funds. If you fail to take this important step, Medicaid could view any money that your parent pays you back as a gift, and this process could create complications with respect to Medicaid's five-year lookback rule.

## 12. What are estate taxes, and how do they differ from gift taxes?

When a person dies, both the commonwealth of Massachusetts and the federal government can assess taxes on the decedent's estate, unless measures have been taken to avoid these taxes. If the estate transfers to a spouse upon the decedent's death, an estate tax will not apply, unless that spouse is not a U.S. citizen.

Gift taxes must be paid when the gift is given, while estate taxes must be paid at the time of death. However, exemptions apply - for instance, if the estate is valued under a certain amount. In 2015, the maximum federal exemption cap was $5,430,000 while the Massachusetts exemption cap was $1,000,000. Massachusetts does not have a state gift tax.

## 13. What is a power of attorney (POA)?

A power of attorney is a document that allows someone else to make financial decisions for you and act as your representative. For example, this individual or organization might handle business matters or financial transactions, settle claims, give donations or gifts, seek professional assistance or buy insurance. Creating a power of attorney document can be useful if your parent struggles with mental or physical challenges.

## 14. What are other types of power of attorney?

- ☐ General Durable Power of Attorney. This document ensures that the original power of attorney remains in effect if needed in the case of physical or mental incompetency, and it becomes valid upon signing.

- ☐ Special Power of Attorney. This type of POA has a narrower focus, and it empowers someone to take care of specific needs, such as real estate transactions, business affairs or debt collection.

- ☐ Health Care Power of Attorney. This tool gives someone the right to make medical decisions for you if you are mentally or physically incapacitated. Do note that a health care POA is different than a living will, which provides specific information on end-of-life decisions.

## 15. What are some situations where power of attorney comes into play?

A. **A serious injury occurs with no warning**. Your parent needs someone to take over a business, pay bills and make important decisions. The POA provides guidance to manage these diverse affairs.

B. **An illness affects your decision-making abilities.** If your parent does not have a POA, a close family member will likely make key decisions that may not be in harmony with his or her wishes. A POA lets your parent stay in control and identify in advance who should carry out what activities and how.

C. **You need to leave the country.** For instance, let's say your parents have planned a 50th anniversary trip to Italy. They've updated their passports, bought their tickets and made hotel reservations. At the last minute, a piece of real estate they've been trying to sell goes into escrow. Instead of postponing their trip, they can assign POA to a representative (e.g. you) to handle the transaction.

D. **You struggle with mobility due to illness or age.** Your parent can assign POA over to an adult child or close relative to do things like manage banking, pay bills and sign documents on his or her behalf.

## 16. What is a health care proxy?

This legal document assigns responsibility to another person to make health-related decisions for you if you cannot do so. For instructions and guidelines - along with a detailed explanation of Massachusetts' Health Care Proxy Law – visit http://www.massmed.org/patient-care/health-topics/health-care-proxies-and-end-of-life-care/massachusetts-health-care-proxy---information,-instructions-and-form-(pdf)/

## 17. What is a guardianship?

If your parent becomes incapacitated or develops Alzheimer's or dementia, he or she will need someone to make important, non-financial decisions.

To that end, you can go through a legal process to establish a guardianship, which empowers a competent adult (e.g. you) to care for your vulnerable parent. Massachusetts law would consider you to be the "guardian" and your parent to be the "ward."

## 18. What powers does a guardian have?

The guardian, who is usually court-appointed, can legally make decisions regarding the ward's well-being, education, health, care and support. However, a guardian does not typically manage financial matters. The guardian handles issues on an as-needed basis and ideally involves the ward in the decision-making process to respect his or her independence.

## 19. Who can petition to be a guardian?

Anyone can submit a request to be a guardian, but the courts consider individuals in the following order:

1. The person listed on the durable POA

2. The person's spouse

3. The person's parent or adult guardian or

4. Any individual that the court deems appropriate.

In order for the court to approve the certificate, a representative for the individual will need to file a medical documentation with the court that details the individual's limitations as verified by a doctor, psychiatric nurse, psychologist or nurse practitioner.

## 20. Does the court have any oversight or other responsibilities to the incapacitated person?

The court will need to appoint counsel for anyone who is in need of guardianship. Within 60 days of appointment, the new guardian will need to submit a report on the ward's condition that details his or her health and future plans for care as well as a summary of all funds and assets in the guardian's possession. The guardian will also need to prepare a similar report at least once a year and whenever so directed by the court. The court will use these plans and reports in order to provide oversight for the ward.

## 21. What happens when a guardian's ideas for care conflict with those of a health-care proxy?

The health-care proxy generally has greater authority to make medical decisions for the ward than the guardian does.

For instance, the guardian cannot unilaterally decide to admit the ward to a skilled nursing facility without a health-care proxy's agreement.

## 22. What are temporary guardianships?

In some cases, an incapacitated individual needs immediate guardianship, if his or her safety is in serious jeopardy. The court can appoint a temporary guardian with limited capacity to serve for a maximum of 90 days or longer, depending on the circumstances.

## 23. What is a conservatorship?

A conservator handles business and property matters for someone with an impairment who cannot make sund decisions even with technological assistance. The court will order a conservatorship only after a petition is filed and after the court conducts a hearing. A conservatorship might include the oversight of specific property or all property as specified by the court.

A conservator oversees only financial matters, while a guardian oversees legal and medical matters.

## 24. Who can be a conservator?

The following individuals can submit a request for a conservatorship: the incapacitated person or anyone invested in the person's estate or well-being, including a parent or guardian, or anyone negatively affected by the person's failure to handle his or her business matters effectively.

The courts will generally consider candidates in the following order:

- ☐ A person previously appointed as the individual's durable power of attorney
- ☐ A conservator with similar responsibilities near where the incapacitated person lives
- ☐ Someone named to represent the incapacitated person
- ☐ The incapacitated person's parent or legal guardian or
- ☐ A person deemed appropriate by the court.

## 25. What does a conservator have the authority to do?

A conservator holds significant power, including the ability to:

- ☐ Make changes to the person's will
- ☐ Give gifts on behalf of the person
- ☐ Operate under the parameters of annuities or insurance policies
- ☐ Oversee the acquisition and sale of property
- ☐ Draft a revocable or irrevocable trust on the behalf of the estate or
- ☐ Handle a power of appointment.

## 26. What are the duties of a conservator?

The conservator has responsibilities as permitted by the court to exercise authority for the incapacitated person. The conservator operates in a position of trust and as such should avoid going beyond the scope of his or her authority. The court will likely request a plan for how the conservator will handle the financial responsibilities of the estate.

## 27. What are the conservator's responsibilities to the court?

Within 90 days of assignment to the incapacitated person, the conservator needs to submit a detailed inventory to the court, summarizing the matters of the estate. The conservator must provide an accounting at least once a year or as directed by the court. Once the conservatorship is terminated, the conservator must submit a final report.

## 28. What are temporary conservators and emergency orders?

The court can enact a temporary conservatorship, which lasts for 90 days, for a person's safety while a permanent petition is pending. The court considers the affected person's well-being and assesses entitlements, businesses and assets when implementing a permanent petition.

SECTION TWO

# Frequently Asked Questions About Elder Crisis Law

*"To care for those who once cared for us is one of the highest honors."*

— Tia Walker

Before we explore more FAQs, let's take a step back and discuss what we call the Four Tenets of Elder Crisis Law(SM). This is a highly specialized multi-disciplinary practice of Gosselin Law. We are the first and only law firm in Massachusetts to practice Elder Crisis Law.

Elder Crisis Law embodies these four key tenets:

**1. Prevention**
Above all, prevention of crisis is our goal. By carefully planning ahead for medical and financial difficulties through document drafting, re-positioning of assets, and establishing

decision-making roles for family members, you prevent the worst impacts of an elder crisis situation.

Prevention takes advanced planning and often giving up control of assets or decision making. We recommend that even in crisis, all family members discuss and implement strategies to prevent further crisis and harm for the elder and other family members. These types of services are normally offered by one of the many "Elder Law" firms around Massachusetts. Elder Crisis Law takes this routine area of law and targets more specifically the immediate risks to the elder and the elder's family.

Prevention areas include:

- Wills, trusts and powers of attorney
- Irrevocable trusts
- Special needs trusts
- Trustee and fiduciary services
- Planning for incapacity

## 2. Response

Crisis is defined as "a stage in a sequence of events at which the trend of all future events, especially for better or for worse, is determined." The key element to shifting a critical trend from worse to better is the degree of response.

Our team approach to every elder crisis situation gives our clients an aggressive, no holds barred counter attack against the negative impact of any elder crisis situation – emergency placement for care, financing long term care, coping with mental health difficulties including advancing dementia, and the pre-death needs of the terminally ill. Through thorough screening and active client communication/involvement we intervene on behalf of clients in crisis by representing their interests with hospitals, nursing homes, medical providers, state and federal agencies, and other third-party providers. Timely, proactive and thorough response to crisis can turn the tide in your favor.

**Response areas include**:

- Applying for MassHealth/Medicaid
- Assistance with nursing home placement
- Protecting your home and assets
- Elder home care and services

## 3. Palliation

There are times when a crisis has reached such a critical point that there are few proactive remedies remaining. It's in these instances that our firm takes a palliative approach to addressing client needs.

Through the use of sophisticated planning techniques and court intervention we can palliate, or reduce, the harm from the inevitable consequences of a crisis. Costs of long term care, guardianship, tax considerations and end of life issues can all be mitigated to some degree by an experienced practitioner of Elder Crisis Law.

**Palliation areas include**:

- Guardianships and conservatorships
- Protecting your home and assets
- Elder home care and services
- Planning for incapacity

## 4. Collaboration

A highly seasoned and experienced team of Elder Crisis Law attorneys is not always enough to resolve a client's crisis. Our clients benefit from our longstanding collaboration with medical providers, hospitals, nursing homes, home care agencies, banks and trust companies, reverse mortgage experts, accountants, Realtors, financial planners, annuity specialists and life insurance professionals.

We do not merely make referrals but work directly as an advocate for our clients with other professionals – assuring our clients the most timely and highest quality services at all times.

**Collaboration areas include**:

- Purchase and sale of real estate
- Trustee and fiduciary services
- Protecting your home and assets
- Probate administration
- Estate litigation

## 29. Why is it important to have power of attorney signed before a senior is incompetent?

Let's say your mother suddenly suffers a stroke, and she can no longer communicate her wishes. How you will manage for her? What kind of authority can you assume? A power of attorney protects both you and her in such a situation and avoids a costly and exhausting legal process.

Ideally, your mother signs the POA while she is competent - for example, before her dementia progresses to a later stage. Once the court deems her incompetent, she can no longer legally sign a power of attorney. Instead, the courts will need to assign her a conservator to handle her financial affairs.

**30. What are Massachusetts Health Qualifying annuities?**
Let's say your mother has been admitted to a nursing home, but your father continues to consult part-time, earning $3,000 per month. His income could negatively affect your mother's eligibility for MassHealth assistance. By leveraging a Massachusetts Health Qualifying (MHQ) annuity, however, he can earn more income per month without risking these essential benefits.

Every year, the state of Massachusetts reassesses the minimum monthly allowance permitted for the spouse of a nursing home resident. This amount - known as the Minimum Monthly Maintenance Needs Allowance (MMMNA) - changes based on the federal poverty level guidelines. Between July 1, 2015 and June 30, 2016, it was $1,991.25. For the previous fiscal year, the amount was $1,966.25.

When basic household expenses are higher than 30 percent of the MMMNA, then the spouse can keep extra money, or the Excess Shelter Amount. This amount could be as high as $2,980.50 under certain conditions. If the community spouse also resides in an assisted living facility, then he or she can seek a hearing and request even more money.

## 31. Why are MHQ annuities important?

Annuities let you defer tax payments while saving cash at the same time. Unlike IRAs or 401(k) s, you do not have a maximum limit imposed that you can donate. This factor matters a lot for someone approaching retirement that needs to catch up with contributions.

As long as your parent leaves cash in the annuity, the money will continue to earn compound interest without being taxed. You can either cash out with a lump sum or receive guaranteed payments over the course of several years or even lifetime income, providing a guaranteed source of earnings during retirement. Annuities offer an additional income stream to complement pension plans and Social Security. They can make the difference between just scraping by and living fairly comfortably.

## 32. What do I need to know about nursing home care in general?

A nursing home provides the most intensive care that a person can receive outside of a hospital. The nursing home will assist patients with personal care, including eating and bathing, along with medical care.

While specific nursing home services vary depending on the facility, they generally include:

- ☐ Room and board
- ☐ 24-hour emergency care
- ☐ Personal care
- ☐ Medication monitoring and
- ☐ Recreational and social activities.

## 33. What's the difference between for profit and non-profit nursing homes?

A for-profit nursing home focuses on turning a profit, while a non-profit nursing home has some type of affiliation, often religious, and accepts residents from varied backgrounds. The non-profit facilities usually cater to individuals from a homogenous group, which is sometimes faith based. These homes are often mission-driven, although they must operate according to effective business models in order stay in business.

The Chicago Tribune cited a 2001 study of nursing homes that showed that for-profit facilities received citations from regulators nearly twice as often as did non-profits. A follow-up study showed that the level of care had not improved much since the first study. Charlene Harrington from the University of California-San Francisco School of Nursing, who authored the report, related that for-profit homes looked for ways to cut costs, such as limiting the number of workers hired and paying lower wages. Both of these strategies negatively impacted patient care.

The for-profit homes also have a higher number of Medicaid patients, which further decreases the quality of care. On the other hand, non-profits limit the number of Medicaid patients they accept.

While you cannot make a blanket assumption that a non-profit nursing home will automatically provide better care for your parent, be aware of these differences as you choose a home for your parent.

## 34. What steps should you take when looking for a nursing home?

Survey facilities in your local area. Investigate nursing home quality. Visit the most promising facilities. Conduct due diligence by asking good questions, investigating references and following up on any concerning reports or observations.

Finally, choose the facility that best meets your needs based on the list of standards outlined below. Once you've chosen a home, actively assess its care on a regular basis, and vigilantly follow up on any reports of potential neglect, abuse or malfeasance.

## 35. How should you assess nursing homes?

First of all, take your time to find the right facility. Many top homes have long waiting lists, so don't delay the search. Planning ahead and giving your parent time to prepare for a move can make the transition less stressful.

Do a preliminary investigation of candidate homes online by reviewing websites and checking for ratings or complaints with the Better Business Bureau. Once you've winnowed your list, visit the facility in person to see whether it's a good fit for your mom or dad. Use this checklist to help you ask the right questions when tour facilities:

- ☐ Is there a waiting period to be admitted?
- ☐ What are the criteria for admission?
- ☐ Do you exclude people with certain physical or mental conditions from the admissions process?
- ☐ Is the facility appearance inviting, and does it have a simple floorplan?
- ☐ Does the facility have handrails, elevators and decent lighting?

- ☐ Is personal property insured?
- ☐ Are rooms furnished or unfurnished? What furnishings should they bring?
- ☐ Can residents choose between single- and double-occupancy rooms?
- ☐ Can they contact someone for assistance at any time from their room in an emergency?
- ☐ Do bathrooms have room for walkers and wheelchairs?
- ☐ Do rooms have telephones? How does long-distance billing work?
- ☐ What level of care does the facility have, and is it what my parent needs?
- ☐ Is the facility's license current?
- ☐ Does the nursing home comply with state safety and fire regulations?
- ☐ Does the facility have specific visiting hours?
- ☐ How does the nursing home handle medical emergencies?

- ☐ Are the administrator and all staff licensed with background checks as appropriate?
- ☐ What is the background of the social workers, doctors, nurses and administrators? Do they have a background and education in geriatrics?
- ☐ Does the staff seem to enjoy working at the facility?
- ☐ How does the staff treat residents?
- ☐ Can the staff help residents if they suffer from memory loss?
- ☐ Does each resident have a written care plan?
- ☐ How often is this plan evaluated, and who evaluates the plan?
- ☐ How often do medical professionals offer checkups of the residents?
- ☐ Does the facility offer three nutritionally balanced meals each day, every day of the week?
- ☐ What is the quality of the meals?
- ☐ Can the facility accommodate special diets?
- ☐ Do the residents have drinking water accessible?

- ☐ Do they eat in their rooms or in a common dining area?
- ☐ Do they have set meal times, or can they eat when they want?
- ☐ Can staff help residents with meals if they need assistance?
- ☐ Do the residents seem content at the facility?
- ☐ What is the reputation of the facility?
- ☐ How is medication stored and dispensed?
- ☐ Can patients take their own medicine?
- ☐ How are additional services, such as speech or physical therapists, coordinated?
- ☐ Can staff help with 24-hour services, such as bathing, grooming, phone calls, mobility, eating and dressing?
- ☐ What type of activities does the nursing home offer?
- ☐ Do the residents seem involved in these programs?
- ☐ How do the fees compare with other area facilities?
- ☐ What types of payment plans are available?

- ☐ Are there different types of services and different fees for each?

- ☐ What services cost extra, and how much are those services?

- ☐ How does the facility handle government payments, including MassHealth?

For further assistance, print out the checklist at: https://www.medicare.gov/Pubs/pdf/02174.pdf.

### 36. What are nursing home resident rights?

Nursing home residents have specific rights, including but not limited to the following:

- ☐ To be given a copy of their rights and medical records
- ☐ To choose their doctors
- ☐ To receive an itemized bill of services
- ☐ To refuse a medical exam without jeopardizing other treatment
- ☐ To keep all medical records confidential
- ☐ To have privacy during a patient exam

- ☐ To have informed consent about treatment and options
- ☐ To communicate freely
- ☐ To complain without fear of reprisal
- ☐ To handle his or her own finances
- ☐ To engage in community, social and religious groups
- ☐ To keep personal clothes and property and
- ☐ To share a room with his or her spouse.

These rights should be posted for public view.

## 37. What if I suspect senior abuse or neglect?

In February 2016, a Massachusetts media outlet reported that the state had taken action against more than 200 certified nurse aides over the past five years for neglect, abuse and other mistreatment of seniors. One of the documented incidents included a cell phone video of someone slapping, boxing and hitting a senior about the shoulder and face. Some of the affected patients suffered from dementia, and they were non-verbal. In another case, a CNA reportedly raped an 85-year-old woman at a facility. The suspect escaped criminal prosecution, although the person — whose gender was not specified — lost a civil lawsuit and was fired.

Another case involved an in-home care worker who stole more than $30,000 worth of cash, jewelry and cherished items from a 90-year-old man. Just 11 days later, after learning the identity of the thief, the elderly man suffered a heart attack and died, reportedly from the trauma of the incident.

Although the accused aides often face criminal charges, they sometimes reach plea deals that include a clean record if they complete probation successfully. The terms of these deals mean that the workers can even return to work, jeopardizing the safety of other vulnerable seniors.

The Boston Globe highlighted the issue in March 2016 when the paper released a comprehensive report on nursing home abuse and neglect after examining financial reports from 2014 from nearly 400 nursing home facilities across the state, including how funds were spent, and documenting safety and health violations.

The Globe's study confirmed that for profit nursing homes, which constitute about 75 percent of the nursing facilities in the state, spend less money on caring for patients than do non-profit homes. One of the issues with funding appears to be the top-heavy salaries of administrators.

The Globe found that for-profit homes spend about 10 percent less than non-profit homes. They also spend about $11 less per day per patient, and they are 60 percent more likely to be cited for safety and health violations.

While many nursing homes, staff and in-home workers professionally care for residents, exercising compassion, those who do not can be subject to civil and criminal lawsuits. Once your parent has been admitted to a facility, keep an eye out for possible neglect or abuse! You might want to drop in unannounced, for instance. If you hire an in-home care worker, secure valuables, and install surveillance equipment.

If your parent suffers an injury or other emergency, call the local police or 911 for help. If the situation is not urgent but you still suspect abuse, contact Massachusetts Adult Protective Services. You can also speak with the long-term-care ombudsman.

You will need to provide authorities with details about the situation and your contact information as well as answers to questions about your parent's health and support system as well as your own observations of any abusive or neglectful behavior. Your report will be treated as confidential. A caseworker will be assigned to the case. Even if elder abuse is not substantiated, APS will provide follow-up services to assist your parent. However, APS cannot force an adult to accept any services, unless he or she has been found to be incapacitated.

If you are concerned about a specific caregiver, you can look up the status of his or her license on the Massachusetts

Health and Human Services Department website. However, disciplinary actions are not always listed on the site.

## 38. What other options does your parent have besides a nursing home?

A nursing home might not be the right choice. Other alternatives include:

- ☐ Home care, which offers assistance with daily tasks and personal care.

- ☐ Home health care, which provides medical treatment or physical therapy.

- ☐ Accessory dwelling units, typically called "in-law apartments," that provide a living and sleeping space along with a kitchen and bathroom.

- ☐ Subsidized senior housing, which allows you to pay a portion of your income toward an apartment, funded by the state and federal government.

- ☐ Home- and community-based waiver programs, which provide subsidies to allow people to stay in their homes or communities.

- ☐ Residential care facilities, which offer help with basic daily activities.

- ☐ Continuing Care Retirement Communities (CCRCs), which provide different levels of housing according to the person's needs.

- ☐ Programs of All-inclusive Care for the Elderly (PACE), which let you stay in the community even if you need nursing home care.

- ☐ Respite care, which provides your caregiver with a break from full-time care.

- ☐ Hospice care, which gives end-of-life support, often in a family member's home.

## 39. What is the Eldercare Locator?

You can call the Eldercare Locator at 1-800-677-1116. This service provides resources for seniors who want to live independently and connections with programs that offer services for older adults.

## 40. How do you qualify for state coverage?

Do not assume that your parent will need to sell his or her home to qualify for MassHealth benefits. MassHealth exempts individuals from selling their homes in the following situations:

- ☐ The person plans to move back to the home.
- ☐ The individual jointly own s the home with another person who lives there.
- ☐ Relatives live in the home.

MassHealth might try to recover related costs by possibly placing a lien against the residence. If your parent sells it, the agency will recoup the costs from the proceeds. If your parent dies with the house in an estate, MassHealth could pursue the estate for repayment of benefits, including nursing home costs.

However, with a long-term-care insurance policy, your parent might not have to pay these recovery costs if he or she lives in a facility and does not plan to return to the residence. This exemption does not include costs of doctor's visits, prescriptions or hospital care, and your parent will be responsible for those expenses.

With or without long-term care insurance, MassHealth will not place a lien on your estate in the following situations:

- ☐ If MassHealth pays for the person's nursing home care
- ☐ If relatives are living in the home or
- ☐ If the person will probably move back home.

MassHealth does not recover costs when real property has to be sold, if the owner has lived there for at least a year and if the person meets certain financial standards. MassHealth will delay collections if any of your parent's children are still younger than 21, if he or she has a totally disabled child, or if he or she has a blind spouse who is living.

## 41. What is the Home- and Community-based Services Waiver (Frail Elder Waiver)?

The Home- and Community-based Services Waiver allows some seniors to live in their residences even if they need nursing-home level care. MassHealth pays for these services to encourage independent living if the benefits cost less. This program saves the government money and gives seniors more flexibility in their care. Your parent can choose from available programs, such as PACE, Personal Care Attendant or Community Choices, depending on eligibility. Family members or assigned caregivers step in to provide care. The person must be at least 65 and must need full-time institutionalization if he or she did not receive this care.

Financial requirements include a maximum income of $2,199 monthly (as of 2015). However, the assets and income of the person's spouse are exempt, so most applicants qualify if they are married. Some individuals might qualify for adult day healthcare, which allows the person to receive services during the day but stay at home at night. Other individuals might receive meal deliveries, transportation assistance and modifications to the home.

## 42. What is the Community Choices program?

Community Choices expands upon the Frail Elder Waiver program and allows participants to move home if they live in a nursing home.

The person must meet one of these requirements:

- ☐ Actively looking for nursing home care within the previous six months
- ☐ Recently suffered a serious medical setback
- ☐ Got discharged from a nursing home in the last month or
- ☐ Faces possible admission to a nursing home because of a lack of support.

In addition, the person must face one of the following risks:

- ☐ Needs round-the-clock care due to health reasons
- ☐ Suffers significant cognitive impairments
- ☐ Cannot manage prescriptions

- ☐ Suffers frequent incontinence or

- ☐ Needs regular help with daily living activities.

Community Choices provides the most assistance of all available programs to participants.

## 43. What is the Personal Care Attendant Program (PACE) program?

The PACE program allows seniors to remain in the community by giving them additional social services and medical treatment. The person must be at least 55, reside in a service area, need the services, be able to remain in the community and agree to comply with the PACE program.

MassHealth does not charge for the services as long as the person meets the financial eligibility requirements, with maximum assets of $2,000 or $3,000 for couples. The maximum allowable monthly income is $2,199. MassHealth coordinates all care, including social workers, aides, therapists and medical treatment. In addition to medical care, the senior receives transportation, in-home services, prescriptions and emergency care 24-7.

## 44. How does someone qualify for PACE?

To encourage independent living, the Personal Care Attendant Program provides disabled and elderly residents in the state with personal care services if they want to stay at their homes. MassHealth pays for the caregivers, but the individuals must be involved in their own care. The senior is an employer who can hire some relatives (not spouses or guardians), neighbors or friends to serve as an attendant.

To qualify, the senior needs to have a permanent disability so that he or she needs assistance with at least two of the following: eating, bathing, personal hygiene or grooming. A medical professional must prescribe the services, and the person must meet the same financial asset limitations as other programs along with the same maximum monthly income. The senior will then undergo a medical exam to see how many hours of help are needed per week. The PCA can help with nearly all personal and daily needs, including transportation. However, a PCA cannot work for a senior who is in a community program paid for by MassHealth or at a nursing home or hospital. The PCA cannot provide entertainment or direct medical services.

## 45. What other programs are available for elders in Massachusetts?

Even if your parent is not at risk for institutionalization, he or she might need help at home. The following programs allow your parent to remain living independently for as long as possible.

**SSI-G and Group Adult Foster Care (GAFC).** These programs help elders transition to nursing homes even if they struggle to pay the prevailing rates. The SSI-G portion pays the person's rent, while GAFC pays for daily assistance. The senior must meet specific eligibility requirements regarding age and financial, health and physical limitations. If he or she has an income greater than the financial threshold, then Medicaid imposes a deductible according to income.

**Massachusetts Adult Family Care.** The Adult Family Care Program allows the elderly person or the caregiver to move into the other person's home in order to receive or give care. Qualifying individuals must have less than $2,000 in assets.

MassHealth pays for 24-hour personal care between $8,000 and $18,000 per year. Legal guardians and spouses do not qualify as caregivers, but you might qualify to be paid as a caregiver for your parent.

## 46. How can you help your parent pay for prescriptions if medicines are still too expensive?

You have several options to help a struggling parent:

- ☐ Try going through the Part D provider for reduced or zero co-pays. Ask the insurance company which pharmacies are recommended.

- ☐ With the approval of your doctor, look into alternative medicines, including generic brands, which can reduce costs by more than 75 percent. In addition, switching to a different brand can also cut co-pay costs.

- ☐ Check into a local discount program through a grocery store or pharmacy that might work with your insurance plan. You can research possible programs online or check to see whether your pharmacist can offer suggestions.

- ☐ In Massachusetts, Prescription Advantage acts as a stopgap measure for those who don't meet the financial requirements for MassHealth but who still have lower incomes. MassHealth only considers income, not assets. For help, call 1-800-AGE-INFO, Option 2.

- ☐ With Medicare Extra Help, qualifying seniors can eliminate or at least reduce copays and Part D premiums by calling Medicare directly.

- ☐ The Veterans' Administration provides prescription benefits to eligible individuals. These benefits can reduce overall costs.

**47. What is assisted living, and for whom is it suited?**

An alternative to nursing home care, assisted living provides room and board to qualifying individuals. These seniors receive help with daily living tasks; however, they generally do not require 24-hour-a-day care. Programs strive to provide autonomy for the senior.

Per The National Center for Assisted Living:

- ☐ About 31,100 facilities across the country provide care for nearly a million people.

- ☐ Half of all assisted living facilities provide care for just four to 10 people. Just 7 percent serve more than 100 residents.

- ☐ Fees vary depending on the location of the facility. In 2010, the average monthly cost was $3,500. Fee structures include all-inclusive rates, fee per service and bundled services.

**48. What regulations cover assisted living in Massachusetts?**

The Executive Office of Elder Affairs oversees all assisted living facilities in the state. The following regulations apply:

- ☐ The facility must be a single or double unit with lockable doors and a kitchenette or access to a kitchen.

- ☐ New facilities must have a private full bath, while existing facilities must have a private half-bath.

- ☐ The senior should receive a personal treatment plan, including payment terms, medication management and on-site staff.

- ☐ The senior should also receive a written agreement with his or her rights, fees, complaint procedures and termination terms.

## 49. What are assisted living resident rights?

The resident has the right to the following:

- ☐ A safe and livable residence
- ☐ Respectful treatment with privacy during exams and treatment
- ☐ Protection of dignity and privacy
- ☐ Private and free communication
- ☐ The use of personal property

- ☐ The ability to engage with medical professionals and community services

- ☐ Management of personal financial affairs

- ☐ The ability to communicate grievances without fear of reprisal

- ☐ Confidentiality of records and

- ☐ Prompt response to requests.

**50. What services does an Ombudsman Program provide?**
A long-term care ombudsman can help you resolve problems with a nursing home or an assisted living facility. This individual can help you compare weaknesses and strengths of nursing homes, talk with residents about living conditions and resolve financial issues.

For more help, contact the Executive Office of Elder Affairs at (617) 727-7750 or 1-800-AGE-INFO (1-800-243-4636).

**51. What is a Continuing Care Retirement Community?**
A continuing care retirement community provides diverse housing options for single and married people, so that they do not have to move from one facility to another if their health or care needs change. Instead, the person receives a comprehensive plan for care from the

facility with a continuum of services onsite. Often, this includes transition to more involved care if a person's health worsens - for instance, if he or she needs to move from assisted living to a nursing home.

## 52. What do Massachusetts Statewide Nutrition Programs offer?

With oversight from the Executive Office of Elder Affairs, the Elderly Nutrition Program provides elders with healthy meals at centrally located facilities, such as schools, churches, senior centers and other locations. Seniors can socialize, take classes, exercise and learn more about their own health. The state offers transportation and, in some cases, meals during the weekends. The program provides deliveries to those who are home-bound. Meals are specially prepared to include one-third of the daily Recommended Dietary Allowance for the elderly.

If you think that your parent might qualify for this program, call the EOEA at (800) 882-2003 for further details.

## 53. What is the Prescription Advantage program?

Any Massachusetts resident over the age of 65 – as well as younger people with disabilities - can participate in the Prescription Advantage program if employment and financial guidelines are met. Seniors qualify if they do not receive prescription drug benefits through Medicaid. However, even someone receiving Medicare benefits might qualify for assistance through the "Extra Help" program from Social Security.

**54. What is the Pharmacy Outreach Program?**

The Pharmacy Outreach Program connects various resources and doctors to minimize the burden of medication costs. The program operates as a public service and interested participants can use this website (http://www.MCPHS.edu/PharmacyOutreach) or reach the program at this toll-free number: (866) 633-1617.

**55. What is the SHINE (Serving the Health Information Needs of Elders) Program?**

The SHINE program provides information to seniors on the often-confusing topics of Medicare, Medicaid, public benefit programs, long-term health insurance, free hospital care, and drug discount cards and assistance programs. Counselors explain benefits, eligibility and rights to participants. They help seniors navigate the challenging path of health care so that they do not overpay for services. They also assist with filling out forms. Seniors can meet with counselors at various public locations across the state, and some counselors will even visit seniors at home. You can contact them at www.MedicareOutreach.org.

## 56. What is the New Dementia Care Standard for Nursing Homes?

If your parent suffers from dementia and must go into a nursing home, you might be especially concerned about his or her wellbeing. Fortunately, Massachusetts law requires health care workers to take eight hours of training and update that training annually. Dementia units also need a "therapeutic activities director" who can provide residents with activities.

These rules ensure that facility workers have the proper training to treat this specialized population. Facilities also must have a fence that surrounds the property for the further safety of residents. They cannot use overhead paging systems, except in emergencies, since these can scare patients.

## 57. What should you know about purchasing long-term care insurance (LTCI)?

LTCI policies can cover one or more of the following: home health care, nursing home care and assisted living care.

Some individuals immediately qualify for MassHealth, or they can move assets easily to become eligible. Others have financial resources to pay for long-term care. Those in between these extremes often benefit most from this kind of insurance.

LTCI policies purchased after March 15, 1999 protect you against estate recovery and pay a minimum of $125 daily for nursing-home care. They also pay for a minimum of two years of care and go into effect immediately without a waiting period or a deductible.

**58. When should you purchase long-term care insurance?** The sooner that you buy coverage; the less the premiums will cost you. For example, your yearly premiums will nearly double if you wait until you are 75 to purchase LTCI instead of buying at age 55. You also run the risk of developing a medical condition that will make it cost-prohibitive if not impossible to obtain coverage. You might opt for less coverage at a younger age and then add another policy later. A qualified professional can help you determine what approach best meets your needs.

Be advised that you will need to pay for LTCI for the rest of your life, and you can pay the premiums for many years without using the coverage. Over time, the premiums rise upon renewal by the insurer - in some cases, rates can spike more than 40 percent. Also, consider inflation protection to be sure that your policy will keep up with the increase in the cost of care. While older policies offered coverage for 5 percent inflation rates, the associated premium costs quickly escalated. By opting for 3 percent or even 2 percent inflation coverage instead, you might cut your premium costs in half.

**59. Where should you go to purchase long-term care insurance?**

MassHealth regulates LTCI policies by setting minimum "qualified policy" standards, and the policies must clearly state if they meet these standards. Search online or speak with a qualified advisor to find reputable insurance companies to provide the coverage that you need.

**60. Who rates LTCI plans, and how do you compare options?**

Respected rating companies include the following:

- ☐ A.M. Best Co., www.AMBest.com, (908) 439-2200

- ☐ Standard and Poor's Insurance Ratings Service, www.StandardandPoors.com, (877) 772-5436

- ☐ TheStreet.com, www.WeissInc.com, (800) 291-8545

- ☐ Moody's Investor Services, www.Moodys.com, (212) 553-0300

- ☐ Fitch Ratings Inc., www.FitchRatings.com, (212) 908-0500

**61. What should you consider when comparing policies?**

Compare and contrast at least three policies in the following areas:

- ☐ Group or individual policies. You can purchase a group policy through your employer with pre- tax dollars, usually at a discounted rate. Under the Division of Insurance, individual policies must meet specific standards, including maximum waiting periods, optional add-ons and a two-year minimum benefit period. Group policies are not regulated as strictly by the DOI.

- ☐ Benefit Maximums. Your LTCI policy will include a maximum dollar amount and maximum benefit amount for a certain number of days. If the costs of your length of stay exceed this amount, you will need to pay the difference.

- ☐ Maximum length. In Massachusetts, benefits might last for your lifetime, for just two years or for somewhere in between. Generally, people purchase about four years of coverage, since the average stay in a nursing home for both men and women is just over two years.

- ☐ Duration of elimination period. Similar to an insurance deductible, an elimination period means that you must pay for your care during a specific time. Elimination periods range from no time to a year and the shorter the elimination period, the higher the premium.

- Consideration of daily living activities. The insurer rates the policyholder's eligibility to start receiving benefits by looking at the following abilities: bathing, moving from a bed to a chair, eating, using the bathroom, dressing him or herself and walking. A doctor assesses the person's abilities; usually eligibility starts when the person needs help with at least two of these activities. Seniors often need assistance with bathing first, so look for a policy that includes this task.

## 62. What information do your parents need when it comes to long-term planning?

Your parents should take the following proactive measures:

- List all debts, assets, expenses, income, will documents, insurance policies, power-of-attorney documents and other relevant information about their plans for care and finances. Keep these materials in a safe place, and make sure a trusted person, such as a close relative or attorney, knows where these sensitive documents are.

- Put a plan in place for emergencies, such as a serious illness. Consider purchasing LTCI or taking out a life insurance policy.

- ☐ Speak with a financial planner, elder crisis lawyer or other professional who can provide you with specific advice.

SECTION THREE

# The Adult Child's Survival Guide: How to Give Good Care and Live Your Life at the Same Time

*"Self-care is not selfish. You cannot serve from an empty vessel."*

– Eleanor Brown

**63. What is the "Sandwich Generation?"**
Social worker Dorothy Miller coined this term in 1981 to describe women aged 30 to 49 who were "sandwiched" between aging parents and young children; these women served as the primary caregiver of both groups. As senior lifespans have lengthened, and as women have put off child bearing, the age of this group has crept up, and men have also joined the club.

About 50 percent of adults in the Sandwich Generation have a parent over the age of 65, and they also raise or support their own children, according to a 2013 report from the Pew Research Center. The Sandwich Generation generally ranges in age from 40 to 65, and about 15 percent of these individuals contribute financially to parents and minor or adult children.

### 64. What are currents trends for the Sandwich Generation?

In 2014, Baby Boomers began aging out of the Sandwich Generation, as their own children from Generation X moved into position. About 31 percent of Hispanics are in the Sandwich, compared with 21 percent of blacks and 24 percent of whites. In addition to caring for their own children and holding down full-time jobs, members of this generation must fend for themselves with no one to care for them. When unexpected hospitalizations or elder care crises enters the mix, extreme stress and overload often follow.

### 65. How should you take care of your children when you're busy putting out fires related to your parents?

Balancing diverse needs related to your children, your parents, your partner, and yourself is neither intuitive, nor simple. Consider doing the following:

**Itemize your needs, your children's needs and your parents' needs.** When your obligations are amorphous, it's hard to prioritize your actions and feel productive. First things first, list out exactly what you need to do (or believe you need to do) on a piece of paper. Itemize everything that comes to mind - from mundane tasks ("I need to get cat litter") to aspirational ones ("One day, I'd love to run a marathon in Antarctica") to challenging ones ("I need to figure out what to do with dad's business mess.").

Once you've gotten everything out of your head and down on paper, you will likely feel a wave of relief. You will see that your project list is not infinite, and you will intuitively get a sense of your priorities. Consider researching and using productivity author David Allen's method for sorting and organizing these "open loops" to get even more clarity and control. This website summarizes Allen's "Getting Things Done" process: http://lifehacker.com/productivity-101-a-primer-to-the-getting-things-done-1551880955

**Draw up a plan.** Former President Dwight D. Eisenhower once sagely observed: "In preparing for battle I have always found that *plans* are useless, but *planning* is indispensable." What did Eisenhower mean by this paradoxical bit of wisdom? The idea is that the *act of planning* allows you to get organized enough to respond skillfully when life's inevitable curveballs come your way. You can better take advantage of surprising opportunities (e.g. an offer from an estranged sibling to stay with mom at the hospital while you travel with your son to his soccer tournament) and deal with out-of- the-blue setbacks (e.g. a medical scan reveals an early stage cancer, complicating your mother's already challenging medical prognosis).

Organize now. Don't put this off. For instance: prepare a living will and powers of attorney. Draw up an estate plan. Investigate long-term care insurance and nursing homes. Reduce risk and stress by thinking several steps ahead.

**Actively solicit help.** An article from Psychology Today offers compelling pointers: "1. Make a list of what you need help with: particular errands, the laundry, some cooking, walking the dog, changing a light bulb, maybe even a shoulder to cry on. 2. Write down the names of friends and relatives who have offered to help, even if their offer was made quite a while ago. 3. Match people with tasks based on their interests, their strengths, their time flexibility and your comfort level with them, given the intimacy of the particular task. A young neighbor may enjoy cooking for you once a week. I read about a woman who gets cooking help from a 10 year old neighbor who has earned her Girl Scout cooking badge.

We have a 12 year old dog walker in our neighborhood. 4. Pick just one thing off the list and contact the person you've chosen. Be direct. So, instead of saying, 'If I only knew someone who could take this coat to the cleaners' ask outright:

'Can you take this coat to the cleaners for me? I'm not well enough to go out.'"

Look to siblings and adult children for additional support. Consider hiring someone to cook or clean or retain the services of an in-home nurse on a part time basis. If you need childcare, hire a babysitter. Look to nearby schools or churches for possible candidates.

**66. What if you live hundreds of miles from Massachusetts?** If you live across the country, and your parents live in Massachusetts, how can you deal with the crisis from a distance?

Data from MetLife/National Alliance for Caregiving indicate that 15 percent of adult children who provide care for parents live at least an hour away, and almost one third provide distance care for someone with dementia. Here are some steps to take to ease your burden:

**Decide on a primary caregiver** - for instance, your sister who lives nearby in Connecticut or a hired helper who reports to you weekly via Skype.

**Get help from the local community** - for instance, neighbors and coworkers can pitch in to monitor your parent's property and check in on him or her.

**Create a plan of action that covers all bases**. Invest the time and mental energy up front to think through your problems, so you're not just reacting to events. Bookmark important ideas in this book or speak with our team to develop a strategic plan.

**Use Theory of Constraints** to determine the obstacles to your goals with respect to managing your parent's situation.

Here's a good primer on this kind of thinking: http://blog.hubstaff.com/business-goals/

### 67. What if your job doesn't offer much flexibility?

Let's say your dad unexpectedly suffers a stroke and needs care, but your demanding job as a school teacher doesn't provide you with flexibility to take time off to help him. Consider the following options:

- ☐ Talk openly with your supervisor about the situation. Communication can go a long way in helping you work out scheduling conflicts.

- ☐ Submit paperwork for the Family and Medical Leave Act. If you have been employed with a company for at least a year, you are legally entitled under federal laws to as much as 12 weeks of time off, as long as the company has at least 50 employees. While new parents often use FMLA benefits for maternity/

paternity leave, you can also use it to care for a senior as well. Additionally, you don't need to take the time off all at once. For example, if you need to take your parent to weekly chemo treatments, you can spread out the available time as needed.

- ☐ Go through your parent's doctor. You will need to submit paperwork to show that you need to use FMLA benefits to care for your parent.

- ☐ Talk to human resources. Your company's HR department might have other options, such as sick leave, personal time or employee assistance, which will give you the flexibility you need.

- ☐ Adjust your work hours. Perhaps you can reconfigure your hours to accommodate your new care needs and/ or telecommute.

- ☐ Hire professional help. A geriatric caregiver or nurse can help coordinate services, review your situation and draft a care plan. It may be financially smarter to invest in great care and pay for that care by working a bit more than to take too much time away from the desk. Be mindful of the monetary value of your time.

## 68. How should you deal with depression, anxiety and other emotions triggered by your parent's crisis?

The following tips can help you take care of your own emotional well-being if your parent's crisis has triggered an emotional response:

**Exercise**. Even a walk for 15 or 20 minutes a day can get your endorphins flowing and boost your mood. Some studies also suggest that safe, slow weight training can improve insulin sensitivity, reduce the risk of problems like osteoporosis and fight back against declines in lean muscle tissue that typically associate with aging. Speak with your doctor before changing your diet or exercise routine.

**Eat right**. While it's tempting to eat on the run when you are in a crisis and default to consuming foods loaded with sugar and refined carbohydrates, consider investing in better habits. Make sure you eat enough vegetables, healthy fats and protein. If you are diabetic or insulin resistant, clinical trials and modern research suggest that a diet lower in carbohydrates may be appropriate.

**Get enough sleep**. If you short change yourself on sleep, you will feel rundown and grumpy. Chronic sleeplessness may create or worsen blood sugar and insulin control, and it can affect your days in surprising ways. For instance, one study done recently in Australia found that sleep deprived individuals (awake for 24+ hours) performed just as poorly on driving tests as did DUI drivers. Prioritize sleep and stay away from too much blue light at bedtime.

**Meditate.** Compelling research suggests that regular mindfulness meditation can be quite effectively at treating depression in some individuals.

**Try a new activity.** Do something different to change up the routine and get your mind off the stress. Read at the park. Volunteer at a homeless shelter. Take a class at a community college. These new activities will stimulate dopamine production in the brain, which can help alleviate depression.

**See a professional.** You have a lot to process. Do not be afraid to seek help and obtain counseling or medication as necessary.

## 69. What should YOU change about your approach to financial and medical planning, based on what's happening with your folks?

As you review each aspect of your parent's situation, make a note to address each topic for yourself as well. While you might need to focus in the short term on your parent's care and get him or her settled into a nursing home or set up with an in-home caregiver, learn lessons from the experience. Organize your own affairs as thoroughly as possible, so that you (and your children) do not face a similar situation when you need care.

Here are a few areas that you will need to address as you plan:

- ☐ Your home. Decide what you will do with your home as you age, especially if you have stairs or if your home is large.

- ☐ Your health. You may need to purchase additional health insurance to cover the gap left by Medicare. Plan for your personal care and talk to your loved ones about your intentions. Options might include home health care, assisted living, or a nursing home. Determine how you will pay for each scenario.

- ☐ Your finances. Review your savings plans to ensure that your assets are protected. Strongly consider setting up a trust and establishing other estate planning tools, as directed by a qualified advisor.

- ☐ Your life. Set up advance directives and powers of attorney, including a living will, to address end-of-life concerns.

## 70. Should you quit your job to take care of your aging parents?

Quitting your job should be a last resort. Before you take such a drastic step, consider both your loss of income and the impact on your retirement.

Answer the following questions:

- ☐ Will you be able to find another job?
- ☐ What would happen to your health insurance and other employer-subsidized policies?
- ☐ Can you apply for Family Medical Leave Act benefits?
- ☐ Will you lose other benefits, such as a potential promotion or significant pay increases, if you quit?
- ☐ Does your employer offer family leave or flex-time that will allow you to care for your parent while keeping your job?

Look at various scenarios before you leave your job.

## 71. Should your parent stay in his or her home?

If your parent sells the home, the prospect of a difficult move looms. Your parent may need to get rid of many possessions and face a confusing, possibly costly readjustment period. Consider the following:

- ☐ **The size of the house, especially if your parent lives alone.** Maintaining a 1,500 sq. ft. home is very different than keeping up a 4,000 sq. ft. home.

- ☐ The presence of stairs in the home, which can be especially difficult for seniors to navigate. If your parent still wants to move, research homes without stairs or other challenging obstacles or maintenance requirements (e.g. big lawns to mow or long driveways to shovel).

- ☐ His or her health and overall mobility. You may need to modify a new home for easy and pain-free navigation.

- ☐ Location. Consider moving your parent closer to you to facilitate care and reduce travel costs.

- ☐ Financial implications. What are the tax consequences? Should your parent buy a new home or rent? Can he or she afford the mortgage and property taxes on a reduced income?

If your parent resists moving, you might back off for a while, but look for opportunities to bring up the subject again. A further crisis, such as a fall or forgetting to pay a utility bill, could help precipitate action.

## 72. Can other family members help out?

Much like caring for children, caring for a parent demands time, attention, energy and finances, stretching your potentially thin resources to the breaking point. If you work full time, and you need to care for your own children or dependents - such as a spouse's sick parent - look for ways to share the burden.

For instance, maybe your siblings live scattered across the country, and you're the only one who's local. Technology makes it easier than ever to connect everyone, coordinate plans, and share responsibilities. Your sister in Seattle can't take mom in for her dialysis, but she can spend 2-3 hours on the phone with insurance company to free up your time.

Another interesting option is to divide projects up by category: one sibling handles the legal and financial issues, while another attends to the medical, social and psychological concerns.

Even if you don't have siblings to help, recruit other family members, neighbors or friends. If even this network is insufficient, look for creative ways to meet your needs and your parent's needs. For instance, hire help, and then take on a second job (at a higher hourly rate) to pay for that help and then some; that way, you can make more productive use of your time.

**73. How can you talk to your parent about sensitive issues?**
No matter your parent's personality and level of openness, you will likely struggle to discuss some of the sensitive topics we've covered. Most seniors cherish their independence, and they do not want to relinquish control.

Be empathetic and be patient. Listen actively, if your attempts to broach the subject meet with resistance, take a step back and regroup. If you cannot mindfully, calmly discuss what needs to be discussed, seek insight from a qualified third party, such as a therapist.

To create some space between you and your parent, consider retaining the services of a geriatric-care manager.

Alternatively, enlist a social worker, case manager or nurse, or contact a professional at The National Association of Professional

Geriatric Care Managers for insight.

Perhaps choose a time immediately following a crisis incident to discuss the bigger implications. Approach the conversation as a matter of concern instead of as a lecture.

Be willing to fight through the uncomfortable feelings in order to broach difficult but necessary topics. Listen to your parent's wishes, document them and strive to follow them.

# SECTION FOUR

# Finding and Working With A Qualified Massachusetts Elder Care Law Firm

*"The time to repair the roof is when the sun is shining."*
(State of the Union Address - January 11, 1962)

– John F. Kennedy

**74. Why should you hire an attorney who specializes in elder crisis law?**
Elder crisis law attorneys know how to advocate effectively for seniors and their family members. They have specific training in a wide range of legal topics that affect seniors, such as

- ☐ Guardianship
- ☐ Conservatorship
- ☐ Medicare/Medicaid

- ☐ Health care
- ☐ Social Security
- ☐ Probate
- ☐ Gift planning
- ☐ Long-term care planning
- ☐ Estate planning, including taxes
- ☐ Advance directives
- ☐ Retirement.

These issues differ from those that concern younger adults - such as long-term financial goals, child care issues, and business structuring and planning.

A Massachusetts elder crisis attorney can also help you triage and deal with urgent, confusing issues. What should you do if you just discovered that dad can't even remember his own phone number or bank pin? What if your mom fell on an icy parking lot and shattered her hip while you're away in California on business? What if your father absolutely refuses to speak with you or your brothers about the state of his financial problems, and you're worried that he'll lose the house and put him and your mother in danger?

Elder crisis attorneys deal with these types of conflicts and scary moments all the time, and they have tested processes and systems for helping adult children get control and develop strategic plans.

They should also be quite familiar with relevant Massachusetts and federal laws regarding complicated topics like patient rights, estate planning, insurance disputes and health care problems.

**75. How should you compile a list of potential attorneys?**
First, determine your standards and priorities. For instance, do you want a local firm? How important is experience to you? What factors would be "deal breakers" for you? To articulate your standards, consider what instructions you would give someone else if you had to delegate the process of hiring an attorney to him or her. That list of standards can help you evaluate your choices.

When canvasing for qualified elder law attorneys, consider asking family, friends and colleagues for referrals. Research online as well. You can also research lawyers by field of practice or Zip Code through the National Academy of Elder Law Attorneys, Inc.

Based on your research and due diligence, narrow your list of prospects down, and then schedule consultations with the most promising law firms.

## 76. What should you ask a potential attorney/law firm?

While this list is far from exhaustive, the following questions will provide you with a place to start:

- ☐ Why does your team do what you do? What inspires you about this work?

- ☐ Who is on your team, and what are their qualifications?

- ☐ What's your process for working with adult children of seniors going through crisis? What kind of service should I expect?

- ☐ Do you only practice elder law, or do you devote your time to other areas of practice?

- ☐ What is your fee structure, and how do you bill clients?

- ☐ Based on the limited information I've shared, what general strategic approach would you be inclined to take?

- ☐ Will you do all of the work on this, or will an associate, paralegal or other staff member handle my case?

- ☐ Should my parent be present during our initial meeting?

## 77. What are some tips for communicating effectively with your attorney and ensuring a successful relationship?

First of all, spend some time getting familiar with the law firm's processes and staff. Ask what you can do to be a good client - what behaviors will be most resourceful. Some attorneys, for instance, enjoy talking on the phone, while others like to work in person or via email or Skype. By understanding what is expected of you as a client - and what you should expect from your team - you'll sidestep problems and enjoy smoother communication.

Unfortunately, your most pressing questions about your elder crisis won't necessarily pop into your head when you're in your attorney's office. Instead, you'll undoubtedly have epiphanies or concerns at inopportune times - when you're in the shower, for instance, or when your toddler wakes you up at four in the morning. Get in the habit of writing these thoughts down, so that you can "batch ask" them to your lawyer, either via email or in person. This strategy should help you consume less of your lawyer's time (thus reducing your fees) and give you some peace of mind, because you'll know that every concern that pops into your mind will be processed effectively.

Finally, be sure to share feedback with your attorney and the law firm staff. If you're confused about what to do next or what will happen with respect to some aspect of your matter, speak up. One of the main reasons for retaining a lawyer to handle your case is so that you won't have to handle your parent's situation all on your own.

**About Our Team**

Throughout life, there are events that require skillful legal counsel. Transitioning a parent to a nursing home. Obtaining a guardianship. Buying or selling a house. The passing of a close relative. These landmark events should cause you to obtain guidance from an experienced attorney.

At Gosselin Law, we center our practice on helping clients with the legal issues associated with these events. We not only respond quickly in times of crisis, but we also help clients proactively prepare for the future.

**Our Philosophy**

John Gosselin set out to form his own firm over two decades ago to provide both the highest quality and most compassionate legal services possible in Massachusetts. Over the years professionals and paraprofessionals who share this vision have joined the practice to form one of the most highly elder-focused law firms in the country. While many clients initially seek our services during a time of crisis, we take pride in the fact that they continue to rely on our legal services at other times because of the trusted personal relationships we develop.

To us, **Elder Crisis Law** means helping people in good times, as well as bad — and building long-term relationships that stand the test of time.

**Professional Guidance**

We believe in being educators as well as advocates. Understanding that you may be dealing with a legal issue for the first time, our attorneys will educate you about your specific situation so that you may feel more confident and secure throughout the process.

**Always Upfront About Fees**

We offer a free initial phone evaluation with a member of our staff. If you decide to engage our services, we will quote all fees in writing prior to commencing any work so that you will always know what to expect.

**Convenient and Accessible**

GosselinLaw offers our clients the added convenience of satellite locations throughout Massachusetts and the Boston area. All offices are handicapped-accessible and evening appointments are available upon request. Statewide in-home appointments are also available in Massachusetts (a service fee may apply).

## Contact Us

To schedule a consultation with Gosselin Law, contact our firm at 781-782-6000.

## On parle français — I μιλούν ελληνικά

MASSACHUSETTS ELDER CRISIS LAW

Do You Need Help Solving Your Massachusetts Elder Crisis?

**Contact us**

Gosselin & Kyriakidis PC
635 Massachusetts Avenue
Arlington, MA 02476

**Phone:** 781-782-6000

www.GosselinLaw.com

**John Gosselin & Darwin**

# Conclusion

*"Do not wait to strike till the iron is hot; but make it hot by striking."*

– William Butler Yeats

Unfortunately, you are in the midst of an elder care crisis that has created enormous challenges - logistically, financial, medical, legal and emotional. This e-book aimed to introduce you to the basics of Massachusetts elder law, so that you can make better decisions and regain a sense of control and clarity about the future. Just to recap, here's what we covered:

**Section One** offered a crash course in Massachusetts elder law. We covered a wide range of topics, including MassHealth, trusts, annuities, capital gains taxes, gift taxes, estate taxes, powers of attorney, health care proxies and beyond, so that you could be conversant with important terms and ideas.

**In Section Two**, we explored common questions adult children have about managing their parents' affairs. For example, we discussed powers of attorney, Massachusetts Health Qualifying (MHQ) annuities, nursing home care, differences between for-profit and non-profit nursing homes, what to do if you suspect elder neglect or abuse and how to qualify for state coverage.

**In Section Three**, the Adult Child's Survival Guide, we discussed practical strategies for handling the complex emotions and transitions you may encounter as you care for your senior parents.

**Finally, in Section Four**, we explored how and why to retain a qualified elder law crisis attorney, discussed questions to ask candidate lawyers, and went over ground rules for how to collaborate well with your legal team. We hope that you have found this guidebook helpful. Whether you need assistance finding an assisted living facility, navigating the Medicaid maze or triaging a complicated, delicate medical situation, we can help. Please call the Gosselin & Kyriakidis, P.C. team for a confidential consultation at (781) 782-6000 or visit our website at www.gosselinlaw.com to learn more.

# Disclaimer

You understand that this book is not intended as a substitution for a consultation with an attorney. Requesting this book or viewing the information in it does not create an attorney-client relationship with Gosselin & Kyriakidis PC or any of its attorneys. To obtain legal advice, please engage the services of Gosselin & Kyriakidis PC or another law firm of your choice. To discuss engaging Gosselin & Kyriakidis PC to help you with your probate or estate planning matter, please contact the firm.

GOSSELIN & KYRIAKIDIS PC IS PROVIDING

" MASSACHUSETTS ELDER CRISIS LAW: HOW CAN YOU HELP YOUR PARENT OR LOVED ONE?" (HEREAFTER REFERRED TO AS "BOOK") AND ITS CONTENTS ON AN "AS IS"

BASIS AND MAKES NO REPRESENTATIONS OR WARRANTIES OF ANY KIND WITH RESPECT TO THIS BOOK OR ITS CONTENTS. GOSSELIN & KYRIAKIDIS PC DISCLAIMS ALL SUCH REPRESENTATIONS AND WARRANTIES, INCLUDING FOR EXAMPLE WARRANTIES OF MERCHANTABILITY AND FITNESS FOR A PARTICULAR PURPOSE. IN ADDITION,

JOHN T. GOSSELIN

GOSSELIN & KYRIAKIDIS PC DOES NOT REPRESENT OR WARRANT THAT THE INFORMATION ACCESSIBLE VIA THIS BOOK IS ACCURATE, COMPLETE OR CURRENT.

Except as specifically stated in this book, neither Gosselin & Kyriakidis PC nor any authors, contributors, or other representatives will be liable for damages arising out of or in connection with the use of this book. This is a comprehensive limitation of liability that applies to all damages of any kind, including (without limitation) compensatory; direct, indirect or consequential damages; loss of data, income or profit; loss of or damage to property and claims of third parties.

You hereby release Gosselin & Kyriakidis PC and the publisher from any liability related to this book to the fullest extent permitted by law. This includes any damages, costs, or losses of any nature arising from the use of this book and the information provided by this book, including direct, consequential, special, punitive, or incidental damages, even if Gosselin & Kyriakidis PC has been advised of the possibility of such damages.

# Do you need help solving your Massachusetts elder crisis?

## Contact us

Gosselin & Kyriakidis PC

635 Massachusetts Avenue

Arlington, MA 02476

**Phone:** 781-782-6000

www.GosselinLaw.com